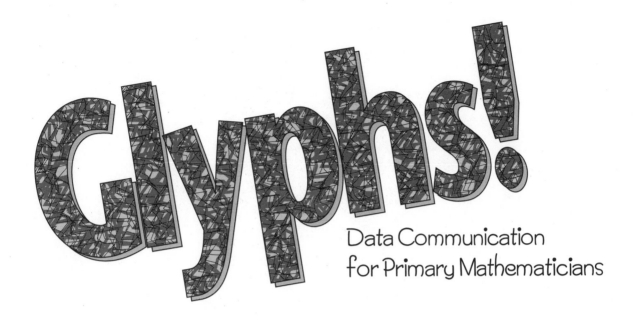Glyphs!

Data Communication
for Primary Mathematicians

by Susan R. O'Connell

Good Apple

Dedicated to
Pat, Brendan, and Katie with love

GOOD APPLE
A Division of Frank Schaffer Publications, Inc.
23740 Hawthorne Boulevard
Torrance, CA 90505-5927

ISBN: 1-56417-663-0

    5 6 7 8 9 MAL 01 00 99

Contents

Introduction

What are glyphs?

Glyphs are an exciting new way for elementary students to collect, display, and interpret data. Similar to ancient hieroglyphics, glyphs are a way of representing data pictorially. Students create glyphs, or pictures, in which each detail represents a unique bit of information. In facial glyphs, the shape of the eyes might represent the number of children in a student's family. The expression of the mouth might represent the age of the child. And the curliness or straightness of the hair might represent the student's handedness. Each glyph has three essential construction elements: the glyph survey (the questions that are asked), the glyph directions (tell what to draw based on the answers given), and the glyph pattern (a reproducible provided in this book or a shape that is hand drawn on a sheet of paper). This unique blend of art and data analysis in *Glyphs! Data Communication for Primary Mathematicians* has made glyphs a creative educational tool that has excited students and teachers in many classrooms throughout the country.

Why use glyphs with elementary students?

The *National Council of Teachers of Mathematics,* in their "Curriculum and Evaluation Standards for School Mathematics," places emphasis on data analysis. Teachers are encouraged to provide students with a variety of experiences in collecting, displaying, and interpreting data.

Glyph activities begin with the collection of data. This is done by means of a survey. In many cases, children gather data about their own lives, making the task particularly meaningful to them. They then follow a series of directions to display the data they've collected. The picture that they create represents that data. Once glyphs are created, there are many interesting ways that students can analyze and interpret them. In the process of exploring their glyphs, students are provided opportunities to communicate their mathematical thinking both orally and in writing.

Along with building data analysis and communication skills, glyphs also stimulate students' mathematical reasoning as they compare, contrast, and draw conclusions from their data. Glyphs can provide opportunities for students to apply previously learned mathematics skills, such as using a ruler to measure the length of arms in the Silly Shamrock Glyph, designing Eggs-citing Egg Glyphs with rectangles or squares, coloring one quarter of a window on their Home Sweet Home Glyphs, or adding the cost of foods chosen on the Fast-food Glyph. Most importantly to your students, glyphs are an exciting and fun addition to your mathematics classroom!

How should glyph activities be introduced to primary students?

Children in the primary grades who are either unfamiliar with glyphs or who may need help reading the survey questions will benefit from a step-by-step approach. To introduce making a glyph, use an overhead projector, chalkboard, or easel. Choose one glyph activity to do as an example. Draw the selected glyph shape for the children to see. Read each survey question aloud, adding your own picture detail to the glyph shape after each question. Seeing the glyph constructed and modeled in this way will help young children visualize and understand the construction process. After the children have heard all the survey questions and watched you use your own answers to create a glyph, the students will likely be ready to begin their own. Provide children with the appropriate construction materials. Go back to the first survey question, reread it to the class, and allow children time to construct the first part of their glyphs. Proceed slowly in this manner, offering assistance as needed. (Note: Many teachers prefer to take the sample glyph away at this time, so that children do not duplicate the sample.)

For students who already have experience in constructing glyphs and who are able to read independently, you may wish to provide the needed supplies and allow students to proceed on their own, reading the survey questions and circling their answers. Children can then construct their glyphs following the glyph directions at their own pace. You will know your class best in determining if these children will need to see a completed sample glyph before beginning work on their glyphs.

5

Why is it important to do additional activities once the glyphs have been created?

Answering the survey questions and representing the data on glyphs are only the beginning of what work with glyphs teaches students. After collecting and representing the data, provide children with opportunities to interpret, analyze, and communicate the data. For example, students could look at other children's glyphs and make statements about the data, such as "Pat likes hamburgers best." (See p. 52.) Ask children to find the similarities and differences between their classmates' glyphs. For instance, they may observe "After playing in the snow, Kevin likes to warm up with hot soup, but Colleen likes to warm up by a fire." (See p. 29.) Give children opportunities to draw conclusions from the data collected, such as "everyone in our class . . . " or "no one likes. . . ." Children will benefit from communicating the glyph information to partners, groups, and the entire class and from expressing their ideas in writing. Most of all, students should have lots of opportunities to share their glyphs and survey answers with others in the class.

How can glyph activities be modified to meet the needs of a specific group of students?

Before beginning any glyph with your class, be sure to prepare ahead of time by reading through the entire glyph, keeping your class's mathematics skills in mind. Do your students have the skills needed to complete the glyph you wish to use? In many cases, a quick review of the skills, such as measurement, identification of different shapes, and fractions, may be all that is needed to allow students to successfully complete the glyph. If necessary, however, glyphs can easily be modified if a question appears too difficult for your class. For example, in the Valentine Postcard Glyph on page 35, if your students have not mastered measuring to the nearest inch or centimeter, simply white out the measurement dimensions and replace them with *small, medium,* and *large.* Provide three sizes of paper for children to choose the appropriate-size piece. If, on the other hand, measuring to the nearest inch or centimeter is too easy for your class, change the measurements to fractions of an inch or decimal parts of centimeters to give them more of a challenge.

Another example of how to modify the glyphs would be to precut some items in different sizes and have students select the correct size. In the Silly Shamrock Glyph on page 38, precutting arms that are 2 inches (5 cm), 3 inches (7.5 cm), 4 inches (10 cm), and 5 inches (12.5 cm) long will provide usable tools for children who are not yet able to construct the arms to the correct size themselves. In this example they may be able to measure the precut arms to select the correct size.

How can students add their own creative touch to the glyphs?

The glyphs in this book are designed for easy and ready classroom use, with simple reproducible patterns provided for you to duplicate as needed. The glyphs, however can be made more creatively by allowing children to design their own patterns on colorful construction paper. Children may begin their glyphs by drawing their own pumpkins, gingerbread men, circles, or squares, for example. Be sure to read the glyph directions carefully when selecting paper for children's glyphs, since paper color is sometimes a factor in designing the glyphs. Using thicker paper, such as construction paper, is suggested when children will be sharing or displaying the glyphs. Students may also show their creativity and personal touch by designing additional survey questions to add to their glyphs. These questions, however, need to be shared with the group so that the glyphs can be accurately interpreted. Keep in mind that creating an accurate glyph based on the survey data and being able to interpret that data are the ultimate goals. (Note: Be sure that students do not make their glyphs difficult to interpret by adding too many creative touches.)

Should parents be included in glyph activities?

Yes! When parents are familiar with glyphs and why we use them, they are better able to help their children. The Parent-Child Glyph, found on page 11, should be sent home when you are introducing glyphs to your class. Along with providing a reinforcement lesson for students, the take-home glyph explains glyphs to parents and offers them a hands-on way of learning about glyphs as they create glyphs with their child.

A second parent-child glyph, Baby Block Glyph, is included on page 12 for an additional home activity. These home activities are enjoyable, interactive projects for parents and children. Helping parents become aware of what glyphs are and how they help students explore data will give them the knowledge they need to reinforce classroom lessons and assist their children at home. For your convenience, a sample reproducible letter to families is provided on page 10.

What materials are needed to create glyphs?

Most of the materials that may be needed to complete the glyphs include, in addition to this book, a photocopier to duplicate the glyph patterns and worksheets, construction paper of varying sizes and colors, scissors, rulers, pencils, crayons or markers in an assortment of colors, glue, tape, laminating plastic (optional), posterboard or butcher paper, and a math or writing journal in which students can record observations and information. The first page of each glyph activity lists the specific materials needed for each student.

How can teachers assess students' understanding of glyphs?

In assessing students' understanding of glyphs, several factors must be considered.

- Are students able to accurately create glyphs from a set of data?

- Are students able to interpret data by looking at a completed glyph?

- Are students able to communicate about glyph data?

In assessing students' ability to accurately create glyphs, ask children to circle their survey responses, and then check the corresponding glyph to be sure that the student has accurately represented the data. In scoring mathematics performance tasks, many teachers prefer a scoring key similar to the one below, where students are evaluated on the degree to which they are able to perform the task.

3—All data is accurately represented.

2—Most data is accurately represented.

1—Some data is accurately represented.

0—None of the data is accurately represented on the glyph.

When assessing students' ability to interpret glyphs, you may wish to use some of the glyphs created by the class or develop your own written assessment tasks. A sample task, based on the Pumpkin Patch Glyph (see p. 21), is shown on page 64 and in reduced form below. In this assessment task, students are asked to look at some to be written tasks. Many of the additional activities presented in this book can also be used for assessment. You might observe group work, assess Venn diagrams, or observe to see that glyphs are correctly grouped or sorted. Whether it is through a formal assessment task or an informal observation, student assessment should be

Pumpkin Patch Glyph

1. Have you ever eaten pumpkin seeds?

	yes	no
stem color	. brown	green

2. Do you like pumpkin pie?

	yes	no	don't know
mouth			

3. Do you like scary or happy jack-o'-lanterns?

	scary	happy
nose	☐	△

4. What is your favorite fall treat?

	caramel apples	popcorn balls	candy corn	other
eyes	△ △	○ ○	▽ ▽	☐ ☐

Now, color your pumpkin.

© 1997 Good Apple

22

Sample Assessment Page
(based on the Pumpkin Patch Glyph, p. 22)

Kevin   Nori   Megan   José
Erica   Miguel   Shamika

Look at the pumpkin glyphs shown above to answer these questions.

1. Which students like pumpkin pie?

2. Explain how you know this.

3. Make tally marks to show the students' favorite fall treats.

| caramel apples |
| popcorn balls |
| candy corn |
| other |

4. Write a sentence about your tally using the word *more*.

5. Do more students like scary or happy jack-o'-lanterns?

6. How do you know?

64

glyphs and answer questions about the data that is represented on them.

Offering students opportunities to write about their glyphs will provide feedback on their understanding of the glyph activities. Assessments, however, do not have

ongoing to monitor student understanding and progress.

Your students will find working with glyphs to be exciting and enjoyable. In the process, they will grow in their abilities to gather, record, and interpret data.

Dear Family,

We are learning about glyphs in math class. A glyph is a way to represent information in picture or graphic form. Like the ancient hieroglyphics, glyphs represent data pictorially. Each part of the picture represents a piece of information.

I am enclosing a glyph for you to do with your child. You'll need two pieces of paper and a pencil to complete the activity. One way to make the glyph would be as follows. Ask your child each question in the glyph survey. Answers to questions can be written down or the answer pictures circled. Next, have your child draw a round face shape on a piece of paper and add the circled face details (eyes, nose, mouth, and hair), following the directions given to create a face glyph. The facial features of the glyph will be determined by your child's answers to the survey questions.

After your child has completed his or her glyph, make a glyph of *your* answers to these questions, using the second sheet of paper. When done, ask your child to make some statements about you by looking at your glyph. Compare the glyph of your answers to the one your child made. What do you have in common? How are you different?

Glyphs can help students gather information, display the information in graphic form, and interpret the information. Plus they're lots of fun! Thank you for helping your child understand glyphs. If you have any questions, please do not hesitate to call.

Sincerely,

_____

Parent-Child Glyph

1. What is your favorite meal of the day?

	breakfast	lunch	dinner
eyes	⊙ ⊙	◉ ◉	△ △

2. What is your favorite afternoon snack?

	cookies	candy	fruit	other
nose	⌒	○	△	○○

3. Would you rather read a book or watch television?

	read	watch TV
mouth	‿	～～

4. Would you rather play indoors or outdoors?

	indoors	outdoors
hair	curly hair	spiky hair

Baby Block Glyph

This take-home glyph is another fun parent-child homework assignment. Children, with the help of their parents, will answer questions about their lives as infants and create building blocks by following the glyph directions.

Materials

❖ glyph survey and directions

❖ building-block pattern

❖ crayons

❖ math journal

Additional Activities

◉ Before sending the glyph assignment home, ask the class to predict the most common answer to each question. Record this information for later reference. When glyphs are returned, tally the answers to see if class predictions were correct.

◉ Have children work in pairs to interpret their partners' glyphs and learn what they were like as babies. Students can then write short paragraphs about their partners from the information learned from the glyphs.

◉ The glyphs and paragraphs from the activity above could be placed on a "Beautiful Babies" bulletin board. You may wish to ask children to bring in photos of themselves as babies to be placed beside their glyphs on the bulletin board.

Baby Block Glyph

1. Are you a boy or a girl?

	boy	girl
design on top of block	ball	duck

2. When you were born, were you bald or did you have hair?

	bald	hair
color of top of block	blue	green

3. Did you have a pacifier or did you suck your thumb?

	pacifier	thumb	neither
letter on front of block	A	B	C

4. How much did you weigh when you were born?

	less than 6 pounds	6–8 pounds	more than 8 pounds
number on side of block	1	2	3

5. When you first came home from the hospital, did you . . .

	cry a lot at night?	sleep well at night?
color of front of block	yellow	pink

6. Did you learn to walk before or after you were one year old?

	before one year	after one year
color of side of block	purple	orange

top

side

front

14

"All About Me" Glyph

This "get-to-know-you" activity is perfect for the start of the school year. Invite children to create face glyphs by answering questions about themselves. Have students begin by drawing a circle on a sheet of white construction paper or by using the reproducible pattern on page 17. The facial features of their glyphs will be determined by their answers to the survey questions. The completed glyphs can serve as a nice introduction to other students in the class.

Materials

❖ glyph survey and directions

❖ white construction paper or glyph pattern

❖ crayons

❖ math journal (for activity below)

Additional Activities

🌀 Collect all the glyphs. Mix them up and give each child a glyph, making sure that children do not get their own. Ask each child to introduce the person whose glyph he or she is holding. By looking at the glyph for information, each child should be able to share some facts about the person he or she is introducing. (You may wish to have children write their introductions in a math journal.) After each child is introduced, the glyphs can be displayed on a classroom bulletin board. A copy of the glyph directions should also be displayed so that viewers can understand the data represented on each glyph.

🌀 The following activity is a good warm-up for "Back-to-School Night" visits by parents and also offers an opportunity to introduce parents to the idea of glyphs. Be sure that children have labeled the backs of their glyphs with their names. Place each child's glyph on his or her desk and write the glyph directions on the chalkboard. When parents arrive, ask them to search the room to find their child's desk by looking at the data on the glyphs. When they think they have found their child's desk, they may turn over the glyph to check the name.

"All About Me" Glyph

1. Are you a boy or a girl?

	boy	girl
eyes	◯ ◯	(eyes with lashes)

2. What is your position in your family?

	oldest	youngest	middle	only
nose	◯	⌒	∠	△

3. How old are you?

	5 or 6	7 or 8	9 or more
mouth	∪	◯	∿

4. How many brothers and sisters do you have?

	0	1	2	3	4
hair	(no hair)	(1 curl)	(2 curls)	(3 curls)	(4 curls)

5. What color eyes do you have?

Color the glyph eyes the color of yours.

16

© 1997 Good Apple

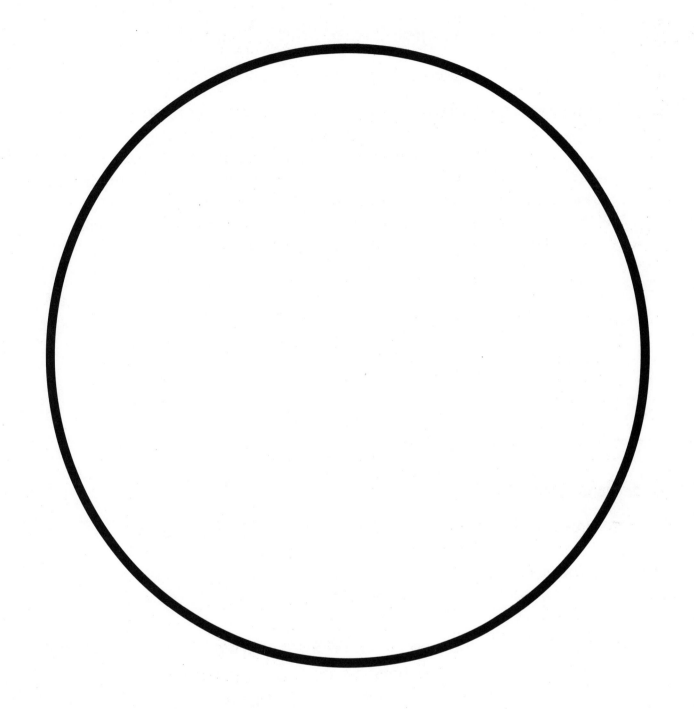

17

Birthday Glyph

In this glyph, children will answer questions about their birthdays and the types of cake, ice cream, and gifts that they enjoy. The children can then create birthday-cake glyphs based on their answers to the survey questions. Photocopy and hand out the cake pattern (see p. 20). Tell children that they will be decorating their cakes with designs that reflect the month in which they were born. The color of the cake icing will be determined by their favorite cake flavor. The children can then add candles and flames to the cake glyphs to indicate their favorite ice-cream flavors and birthday gifts.

Materials

❖ glyph survey and directions

❖ cake pattern

❖ crayons

❖ math journal (for activity below)

Additional Activities

☺ Create a class birthday graph by placing month headings across the top of a large bulletin board or chalkboard. Ask students to tape their glyphs under the correct headings, beginning at the bottom of the board as one would when making a bar graph. Have students look at the completed graph to find out answers to questions such as the following.

Which month has the most birthdays? The fewest birthdays?

Are there any months that have the same number of birthdays?

☺ Ask students to write in their math journals about the class birthday graph. What information does it show? Encourage them to use terms like *most, least, more than, less than,* and *equal to* in their writing.

18

Birthday Glyph

1. In which month were you born?

Decorate the side of your cake with the design for the month you were born.

January—snowmen	July—suns
February—hearts	August—fish
March—shamrocks	September—apples
April—umbrellas	October—pumpkins
May—kites	November—leaves
June—boats	December—trees

2. What is your favorite kind of ice cream?

	vanilla	chocolate	chocolate chip	other
number of candles	1	2	3	4

3. What is your favorite kind of cake?

	chocolate	yellow	other
color of icing	brown	yellow	blue

4. Which birthday gift would you rather receive?

	clothes	toys
candle flame	red	yellow

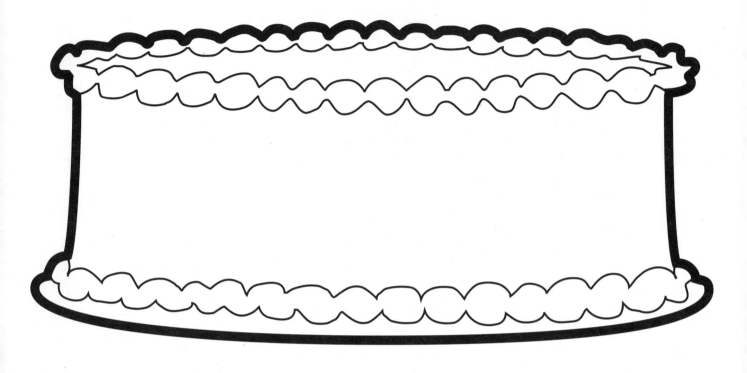

 20

Pumpkin Patch Glyph

This is a good glyph to use in the fall. Children may begin by drawing pumpkin shapes on pieces of white construction paper or by using the pumpkin pattern on page 23. Have children answer the questions about pumpkins and autumn treats to determine the features of their jack-o'-lanterns. If you wish, completed glyphs may be cut out.

Materials

❖ glyph survey and directions

❖ pumpkin pattern or white construction paper

❖ crayons

❖ scissors

Additional Activities

⑥ Create a pumpkin patch by designating a section of the classroom floor where children can place their pumpkin glyphs. Next, call on individual students to go pumpkin picking. Give specific directions, such as *Katie, can you pick a pumpkin that was made by someone who likes scary jack-o'-lanterns?* or *José, can you pick a pumpkin made by someone who has not eaten pumpkin seeds?* The student pumpkin-pickers should be able to explain how they decided on the pumpkins they chose from the pumpkin patch.

⑥ For the activity above, several smaller pumpkin patches could be set up in different areas of the classroom to allow groups of students to go pumpkin picking at the same time. As you give a direction, a student from each group is selected to find a pumpkin in his or her patch.

Pumpkin Patch Glyph

1. Have you ever eaten pumpkin seeds?

	yes	no
stem color	brown	green

2. Do you like pumpkin pie?

	yes	no	don't know
mouth			

3. Do you like scary or happy jack-o'-lanterns?

	scary	happy
nose		

4. What is your favorite fall treat?

	caramel apples	popcorn balls	candy corn	other
eyes				

Now, color your pumpkin.

Thanksgiving Placemat Glyph

In this glyph, children answer questions about Thanksgiving food and activities and use the data to make placemats. Students' answers to the first question determine the color of construction paper to use for their glyphs. The paper will be divided into four quadrants. Have children place the appropriate data in the quadrant that is highlighted on the glyph survey. (See p. 25.) Note: You may wish to have students draw a vertical and a horizontal line at what they estimate to be halfway across and halfway up or down to divide the paper into four quadrants. Students could also fold their papers in half vertically and horizontally to create fold marks showing the quadrants, or use their ability to visually identify each quadrant without the aid of lines.

Materials

◆ glyph survey and directions

◆ 12" x 18" (30 cm x 45 cm) construction paper—
  yellow, orange, green, and white

◆ crayons or markers

◆ writing paper (for activity below)

◆ laminating material (for activity below)

Additional Activities

Have children work with partners to write a few more questions to add additional data to the glyphs.

Children can use the information on their placemats and questions designed with their partners (see activity above) to write paragraphs describing the perfect Thanksgiving. Paragraphs could be glued to the backs of the placemats and the placemats laminated and sent home as Thanksgiving gifts for family members.

Thanksgiving Placemat Glyph

1. What is your favorite Thanksgiving main dish?

	turkey	ham	duck	other
color paper	yellow	orange	green	white

2. What is your favorite meal of the day?

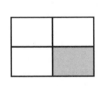

breakfast	lunch	dinner

3. What is your favorite corn dish?

on the cob	off the cob	popcorn	other

4. What is your favorite Thanksgiving Day activity?

watching a parade	watching football	eating	playing with friends

5. Do you like to spend Thanksgiving at your house or at someone else's house?

your house	someone else's house

Create a border to decorate your placemat.

Gingerbread Man Glyph

To create Gingerbread Man Glyphs, have children answer the questions on page 27 about cookies. Then, using the gingerbread man patterns, invite children to add details based on the data they collected. (Note: For survey questions #3 and 4, children will need to draw a nose and bow tie of their choice before adding color to answer the questions. In question #5, students can create their own button design, then draw in one or two buttons to indicate their answers.)

Materials

❖ glyph survey and directions

❖ gingerbread man pattern

❖ crayons or markers

❖ math journals (for activity below)

Additional Activities

⊙ Have children work in small groups. Place in the center of each group a few of the glyphs made by students. Invite children to decide on a way to sort the glyphs based on the glyphs' attributes—for example, gingerbread men with one or two buttons, gingerbread men with black, blue, green, or red noses, and so on. After groups have decided how to sort their glyphs, each should decide on a name for the group, such as Milk Drinkers, Juice Drinkers, or Water Drinkers. Have groups share their method of sorting and categorizing with the class.

⊙ Using their math journals, have students write descriptions of how their groups sorted and categorized their glyphs.

Gingerbread Man Glyph

1. What is your favorite kind of cookie?

eyes	chocolate chip	oatmeal	sugar	other
	⊙ ⊙	● ●	◑ ◑	— —

2. When is your favorite time to eat cookies?

mouth	at lunch	after school	after dinner
	‿ (smile)	∪	○

3. What do you like to drink with your cookies?

	milk	juice	water	other
nose color	black	blue	green	red

4. When you eat cookies, how many do you usually eat?

	1 or 2	3 or 4	5 or more
color of bow tie	red	purple	orange

5. Are cookies your favorite snack?

	yes	no
number of buttons	1	2

28

For a wintertime glyph activity, have children make Snowman Glyphs. Students can construct glyphs based on their feelings about snow and what they like to do in the snow. To begin, have children draw two circles on sheets of white paper, or distribute copies of the reproducible pattern on page 31.

Materials

- ❖ glyph survey and directions
- ❖ snowman pattern or white paper
- ❖ crayons or markers
- ❖ math journals (for activity below)
- ❖ tape (for activity below)

Additional Activities

⑥ Draw a very large Venn diagram on the chalkboard. (See below for an example.) Label one circle *Loves snow* and the other one *Toes get cold first*. Invite children to come to the chalkboard and tape their snowmen in the correct place on the diagram according to their feelings about winter. Ask children, *How many snowmen are in the center of the diagram where the two circles overlap?* (loves snow **and** toes get cold first) *How many snowmen are outside the diagram's circles?* (Neither fact is true for them.) Have students write in their math journals about what the diagram shows.

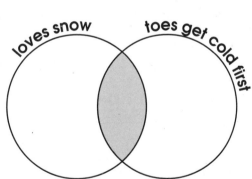

⑥ Challenge students to add a third circle to the Venn diagram. Be sure that each circle represents a response from a different survey question.

Snowman Glyph

1. Do you like snow?

mouth	no, don't like snow	yes, like snow	yes, love snow!
	⌢	⌣	☺

2. What is your favorite snowy day activity?

hat	sledding	throwing snowballs	building snow forts	making snowmen
	🎩	⛑	△	⬚

3. How long do you like to stay out in the snow?

arms	less than 30 minutes	30 minutes or more
	○	○

4. What is the first part of your body that gets cold in the snow?

number of buttons	toes	nose	fingers	ears
	1	2	3	4

5. How do you like to warm up after being in the snow?

nose	drink hot cocoa or soup	sit by the fire	wrap up in a blanket	other
	◯	☐	⬭	△

6. Now, finish your snowman with eyes the same color as yours!

30

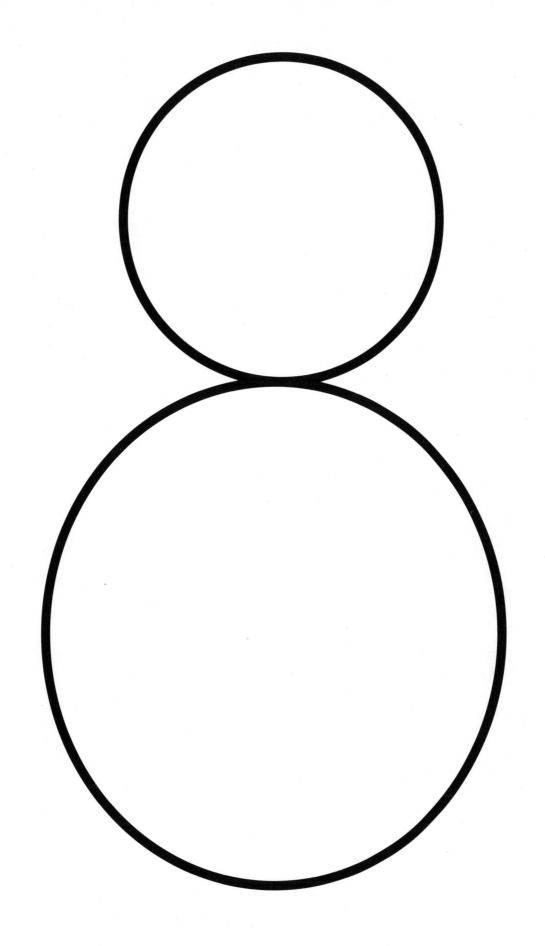

Bookworm Glyph

To focus on children's love of reading, have them create Bookworm Glyphs. Begin by having children answer the questions on page 33 about reading. Next, have each child cut out a bookmark pattern and make a design on the bookmark by following the directions for the glyph. After finishing the glyphs, you may wish to encourage students to add fancy borders or backgrounds to their bookmarks, such as a sun, grass, and trees.

Materials

- ❖ glyph survey and directions
- ❖ bookmark pattern
- ❖ scissors
- ❖ crayons
- ❖ children's favorite books (for activity below)

Additional Activities

⑥ Pair students and have them switch glyphs with their partners. Ask children to "read" their partner's glyphs and follow your directions (see below for suggestions).

- Stand if your partner likes to read with someone else.

- Raise your hand if your partner likes to read in bed.

- Put your hands on your head if your partner's favorite time to read is the morning.

- Clap your hands if your partner reads more at home than at school.

⑥ Pause after each direction and ask children how they know that their responses are true for their partners. (Students should respond with statements like *because the bookworm has a smiley face.*)

⑥ Pass out children's favorite books and give students a few minutes to share one with their partners.

Bookworm Glyph

1. Do you like to read books?

	yes	no
draw a bookworm with	4 circles	5 circles

2. Would you rather read with someone or read all by yourself?

	read with someone	read alone
antennae		

3. Where do you read more?

	school	home
mouth		

4. Do you like to read in bed?

	yes	no
eyes		

5. When is your favorite time to read?

	morning	afternoon	evening
color of bookworm	blue	green	purple

Valentine Postcard Glyph

Candy is a favorite gift on Valentine's Day. Have students create valentine postcards to give to friends by answering questions about candy. Provide each child with a sheet of construction paper measuring 6" x 10" (15 cm x 25 cm) or a copy of the reproducible pattern on page 37. Based on their answers to the first question, students may need to cut their papers to a shorter length.

Materials

❖ glyph survey and directions

❖ 6" x 10" (15 cm x 25 cm) white construction paper or glyph pattern

❖ crayons

❖ scissors

❖ ruler

❖ posterboard (for graph activity below—one per group)

❖ math journals (for activity below)

Additional Activities

Display glyphs on the chalkboard ledge or on a bulletin board. Working in groups, have students select a question from the glyphs, such as *Which saying describes you best?* and create graphs to show the class's data for that question. Remind groups to add titles and labels to their graphs. Ask groups to present their graphs to the class.

After all the graphs have been presented, ask students to select a graph and write in their math journals three sentences describing the information on the graph.

When class activities are completed, students can turn their glyphs into postcards to give to friends. On the backs of the glyphs, students can write short messages explaining what the glyphs mean. Then have students add addresses and draw stamps and the glyph postcards are ready to give to friends!

Valentine Postcard Glyph

1. What is your favorite kind of valentine candy?

	chocolate	cinnamon hearts	conversation hearts
size of postcard	6" x 8" 15cm x 20cm	6" x 9" 15cm x 22.5cm	6" x 10" 15cm x 25cm

2. How often do you eat candy?

	a lot	sometimes	never
draw hearts on your postcard	4 hearts	3 hearts	2 hearts

3. What is your favorite filling for chocolate candy?

	coconut	nuts	caramel	peanut butter
design on hearts	♡	♡	♡	♡

4. It's fun to read the sayings on conversation hearts. Which saying describes you best?

Color the background to match your choice.

"Red Hot"	—	red background
"Cool Dude"	—	blue background
"Too Cute"	—	pink background
"Smart Cookie"	—	purple background

Color the hearts any color you'd like!

36

6" / 15 cm

Centimeters 1 2 3 4 5 6 7 8 9 10 11 12 13 14 15 16 17 18 19 20 21 22 23 24 25

Inches 1 2 3 4 5 6 7 8 9 10

Silly Shamrock Glyph

Many people like to wear green or orange on St. Patrick's Day. Have students answer the questions on page 39 about the color green. Their answers will help them create funny shamrock people. Ask children to carefully cut out the shamrock and hat patterns (see p. 40) and glue the shamrocks onto construction paper. Next, have children measure out two arms from the 1-inch (2.5 cm) strips of paper. (The length of the arms is determined by their answers to the question on favorite vegetables.) Invite children to cut the arms out and glue them onto the shamrocks. Then they may glue the hats onto the shamrock heads. Encourage children to use crayons to add facial features, hats, and shoes.

Materials

❖ glyph survey and directions

❖ shamrock and hat patterns

❖ construction paper

❖ one 1" (2.5 cm) wide strip of paper at least 10" (25 cm) long

❖ ruler

❖ crayons or markers

❖ glue or tape

❖ scissors

❖ writing paper (for activity below)

Additional Activities

Put completed shamrock glyphs on the chalkboard ledge. Ask students to answer the following questions, using the glyphs for information.

- How many students are wearing something green today?

- How many students have green eyes?

- Are there any students who are wearing green and have green eyes?

Arrange children in small groups and have them write questions, like those above, for the class to solve. You may wish to select one of the questions for students to solve in writing or to have children select a question. Have children write about the strategy used to solve the problem (for example, a Venn diagram, sorting and counting, and so on).

Silly Shamrock Glyph

1. Do you have green eyes?

	yes	no
eyes	◉ ◉	⊙ ⊙

2. What is your favorite shade of green?

	kelly	neon	pastel
mouth	‿	—	∼∼

3. What is your favorite green vegetable?

	peas	green beans	broccoli	other
length of arms	2'' (5 cm)	3'' (7.5 cm)	4'' (10 cm)	5'' (12.5 cm)

4. What is your favorite green candy?

	M&M's	jelly beans	gumdrops	other
hat				

5. Are you wearing something green today?

	yes	no
shoes	red	black

40

"Eggs-citing" Egg Glyph

Students will enjoy creating decorated "Eggs-citing" Egg Glyphs. Have them begin by cutting oval shapes from construction paper or by using the egg pattern on page 43. Invite children to add decorations and designs (one at a time) to their egg patterns, based on their answers to the glyph questions. After designing their eggs, students can have a classroom egg hunt! (See below.)

Materials

❖ glyph survey and directions

❖ construction paper or egg pattern

❖ crayons

❖ scissors

❖ Egg Hunt Worksheet, on page 44

Additional Activities

In this activity, students use the data represented on the glyphs to go on an egg hunt. Have students write their names on the fronts of the glyphs and place the glyphs on their desks. Give students a copy of the Egg Hunt Worksheet, and ask them to move silently throughout the classroom, looking for children's names to complete their worksheets. Each time they find an egg that fits the egg hunt directions, they should write on the worksheet the name found on the egg. Have children return to their seats as they complete the egg hunt. Check students' answers by having each child stand when his or her name could be an answer to one of the worksheet questions.

Challenge students to find out the total number of children whose favorite way to eat eggs is *scrambled, hard-boiled, fried,* and *no favorite way.* Have them create a tally sheet or graph the results, then determine which are the most and least favorite ways of eating eggs.

"Eggs-citing" Egg Glyph

1. Have you ever cracked open an egg all by yourself?

	yes	no
mouth	⌣	～

2. About how many eggs do you eat each week?

	0	1–3	4 or more
eyes	• •	⌒ ⌒	◖ ◗

3. What is your favorite breakfast food made with eggs?

	waffles	pancakes	French toast	other
nose	⌒	◯	△	∠

4. What is your favorite dessert made with eggs?

	cake	brownies	cookies	other
egg design	circles	triangles	squares	rectangles

5. What is your favorite way to eat eggs?

	scrambled	hard-boiled	fried	no favorite way
egg color	pink	purple	yellow	blue

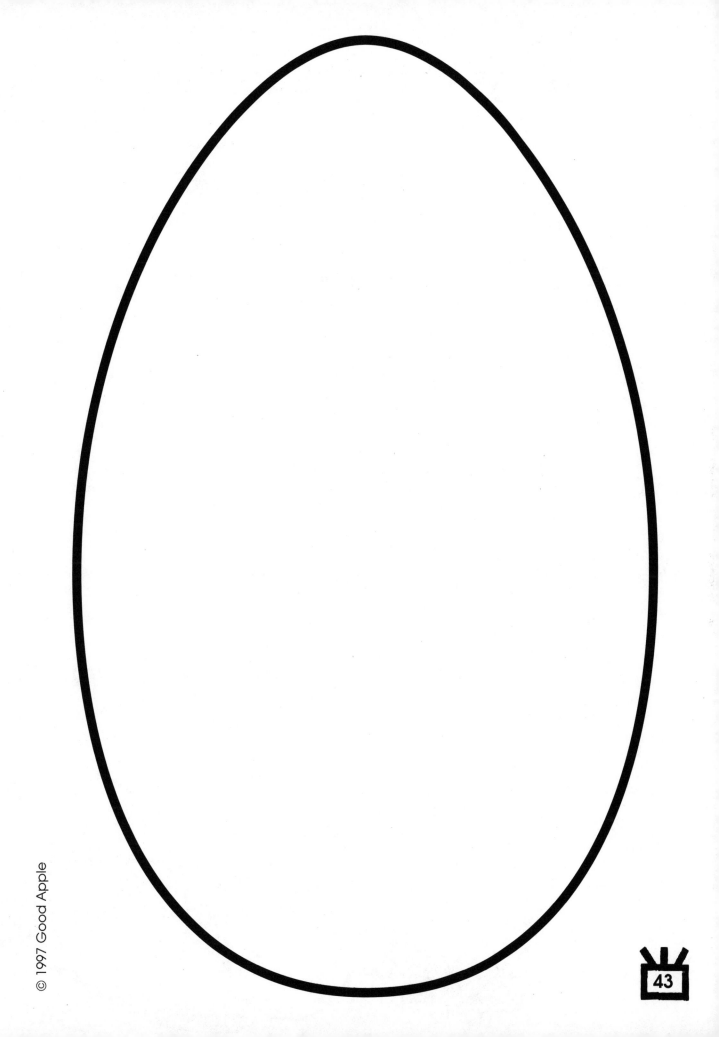

43

"Eggs-citing" Egg Hunt

1. _____ likes scrambled eggs best.

2. _____ likes cake best for dessert.

3. _____ eats four or more eggs each week.

4. _____ has cracked an egg open without help.

5. _____ likes waffles best for breakfast.

6. _____ likes pancakes best for breakfast and likes cookies best for dessert.

Rainy Day Glyph

For a rainy day theme, have students create these special glyphs. Give children copies of the reproducible umbrella pattern (see p. 47) and invite them to add handles, knobs on top, and designs based on their answers to the survey questions to create their very own Rainy Day Glyphs.

Materials

❖ glyph survey and directions

❖ umbrella pattern

❖ crayons or markers

❖ Puddle Tally and Graph Worksheet, on page 48 (for activity below)

❖ math journals (for activity below)

Additional Activities

⊙ Students can create bar graphs with the Puddle Tally and Graph Worksheet, showing what classmates do when they see a puddle. Before they gather their responses, encourage students to predict what they think most of their classmates do. Have children use tally marks in the Puddle Tallies to collect information for the graphs. Children can then complete the Puddle Graphs by using the tally information. Ask children to orally compare the results of their Puddle Tallies and Graphs with their predictions.

⊙ Invite students to write in their math journals about the preceding activity and its results. Younger students may benefit from using slotted sentences such as, *I predicted that . . . , My graph shows that. . . .*

Rainy Day Glyph

1. Do you like rainy days?

	yes	no
knob on umbrella	◯	△

2. When you see a puddle, what do you do?

	step in it	go around it	jump over it
handle	⌓		⌓

3. What is your favorite rainy day activity?

	watching TV	reading a book	playing a game	other
umbrella design				

4. Have you ever played outside in the rain?

	yes	no
color of umbrella	yellow	orange

What We Do When We See a Puddle

Puddle Tally

Step in it	
Go around it	
Jump over it	

Puddle Graph

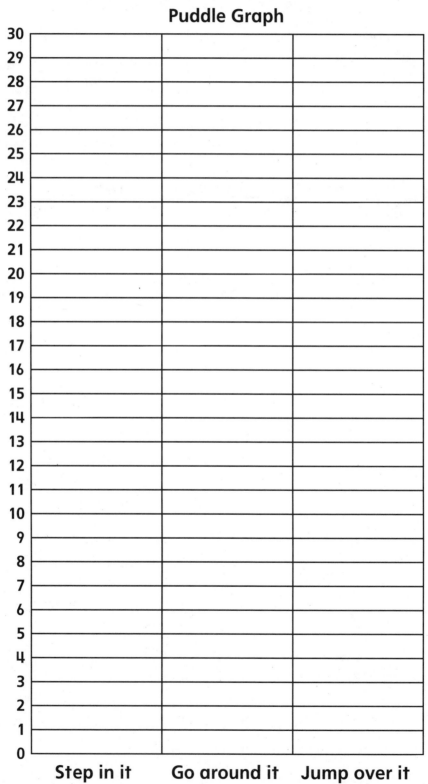

Number of Students

	Step in it	Go around it	Jump over it

Home Sweet Home Glyph

Invite children to create special glyphs about their homes. Have children begin by choosing the correct shapes for their glyphs (see p. 51 for patterns) by answering the first question in the survey on page 50. After they add design details to their glyphs, have children cut the glyphs out.

Materials

❖ glyph survey and directions

❖ home patterns

❖ crayons

❖ scissors

❖ butcher paper or posterboard (for each group in activity below)

❖ glue sticks (for activity below)

❖ math journals (for activity below)

Additional Activities

⟴ Invite students to work in small groups to create maps, using large pieces of butcher paper or posterboard and their glyphs. Have students follow these directions.

1. Draw a compass rose on your map.
2. Draw three main streets on your map and label them.
3. Create a legend with symbols for a playground, school, lake, and park. Use the symbols to place these items on your map.
4. Decide on locations in which you would like to live, and glue your home glyphs on the map at these places.
5. Decide on a name for your community and write the name at the top of the map.

⟴ After they have created their maps, ask students to calculate the number (or fraction) of homes in their communities that have pets or the number (or fraction) of homes that have eight or more people living in them. Have students write in their math journals about the strategies used to answer these questions.

⟴ Have students discuss as a class, or in small groups, whose home is closest to and farthest from certain landmarks (such as a school or a park). Or ask students to write in their math journals directions for traveling from one location to another.

Home Sweet Home Glyph

1. Do you live in a house, townhouse, or apartment?

	house	townhouse	apartment
shape of glyph	square ☐	rectangle ▭	rectangle ▯

2. How many bedrooms are in your home?

	1	2	3 or more
number of windows	1	2	3

3. Do you have a fireplace?

	yes	no
shape of door	rectangle	triangle

4. How many people live in your home (including you)?

	2–4	5–7	8 or more
shade each window	$\frac{1}{4}$	$\frac{1}{2}$	$\frac{3}{4}$

5. Do any pets live with you?

	yes	no
shape of roof		

51

Fast-food Glyph

Children will enjoy creating glyphs of their favorite fast foods. To create the glyphs, invite students to imagine that they are ordering from their favorite fast-food restaurants. As students answer the survey questions, they will be selecting main items, drinks, and desserts, and deciding if they will eat in or carry out. Their answers will create glyphs in the form of fast food drinks. After designing the cups, students can decorate and cut them out, then glue on straws by following the glyph directions. Money skills can also be reinforced with the activity below.

Materials

❖ glyph survey and directions
❖ cup and straw patterns
❖ crayons
❖ scissors
❖ glue
❖ Fast-food Price List, on page 55 (for activity below)
❖ calculator or coin manipulatives (for activity below)

Additional Activities

⑥ After making glyphs, ask children to calculate the cost of the food ordered, using copies of the Fast-food Price List and calculators or coin manipulatives. (Note: For young students the cost of the food items can be changed to match their counting skills.) Create a large money number line ranging from $0.00 to $2.50 on a chalkboard or large bulletin board. After figuring out the cost of the order, each child can place his or her glyph on the number line at the spot that shows the cost of the meal. Children will then be able to see the range of prices for the meals ordered. (Note: If calculators are used, you may need to review how to enter money amounts using a decimal point.)

⑥ For an added challenge, have the class determine the least and most expensive meals.

Fast-food Glyph

Select a mouth-watering meal from these fast-food items.

1. What would you order?

design on cup	hamburger	cheeseburger	chicken	taco
	○ ○ ○	□ □ □	△ △ △	◗ ◗

2. What would you like to drink?

color of cup	cola	orange	lemon-lime	milkshake
	blue	orange	green	brown

3. What would you like for dessert?

place for straw	cookies	ice cream	pie
	right side of cup	left side of cup	center

4. Would you rather eat-in or carry-out?

straw design	eat-in	carry-out
	(striped straw)	(plain straw)

Fast Food

-Main Items-

Hamburger   50¢
Cheeseburger   60¢
Chicken   80¢
Taco   70¢

-Drinks-

Cola   50¢
Orange   50¢
Lemon-lime   50¢
Milkshake   80¢

-Desserts-

Cookies   35¢
Ice Cream   65¢
Pie   55¢

Ladybug Glyph

Focus on children's curiosity about insects with the Ladybug Glyph. Have children answer the survey questions (see p. 57) regarding their feelings about bugs and their experiences with them. Students can then create ladybug glyphs (see p. 58 for pattern) using their survey answers.

Materials

❖ glyph survey and directions

❖ ladybug pattern

❖ crayons or markers

❖ ruler

❖ writing paper or math journals (for activity below)

Additional Activities

Invite children to discuss and then decide on a strategy for figuring out the class's least favorite bug. Children may decide to take a vote, do a class graph, sort the glyphs, or line students up based on their least favorite bug. Any strategy that is organized and will result in gathering the needed information is acceptable.

Have children write stories using topics such as

- their least favorite bug,

- the time they were bitten or stung by a bug,

- the bug they caught.

The stories may be real or make-believe.

Ladybug Glyph

1. Are you afraid of bugs?

	yes	no
antennae		

2. Have you ever caught a bug?

	yes	no
length of 6 legs	2" (5 cm)	3" (7.5 cm)

3. Have you ever been bitten or stung by a bug?

	yes	no
number of dots on right side	2	3

4. What is your least favorite kind of bug?

	mosquito	fly	bee	other
number of dots on left side	1	2	3	4

5. Would you hold a ladybug?

	yes	no
color of bug's body	red	orange

6. If you think making glyphs is fun, draw a happy face on your ladybug. If you don't like making glyphs, give your ladybug a sad face.

Summer Sunshine Glyph

Children may enjoy making glyphs that tell about their favorite summer drinks, fruits, and places to play. Begin by having students draw a large circle on white construction paper or use the pattern on page 17. Then have children answer the survey questions on page 60 and add their designs and colors to create their Summer Sunshine Glyphs.

Materials

❖ glyph survey and directions

❖ white construction paper or pattern on page 17

❖ crayons or markers

Additional Activities

◉ Have children stand and hold their glyphs. In an open space, group children to form two circles, one inside the other. Each circle should have the same number of children in it. (If there is an odd number of students in the class, you should join in.) Invite students to walk slowly in the circles, with the inner circle walking clockwise and the outer circle walking counterclockwise. When you say the word *shine,* children stop walking. Students who are standing across from each other now become partners. Partners share their glyphs to see in how many ways they are alike.

◉ You may wish to repeat the moving circles in the activity above so that children can share their glyphs with new partners. As a bonus you may wish to give treats to the first two partners who find their glyphs to be alike in all ways.

Summer Sunshine Glyph

1. Do you like picnics?

	yes	no
rays	⚙	☀

2. Where is your favorite place to play in the summer?

	indoors	outdoors
eyes	👀	⌒ ⌒

3. What is your favorite cool summer drink?

	lemonade	soda pop	iced tea	milk	water
mouth	‿	o—o	∿	‿ (smile)	◯

4. What is your favorite summer fruit?

	watermelons	peaches	strawberries	other
sun color	yellow	orange	pink	purple

Decide on the Survey Questions

To enable students to create their own School Year Memories Kite Glyphs, you will need to decide on survey questions that would lead to a discussion of the school year. You might ask students which assemblies, field trips, or holiday parties they liked best. Or ask children to write on sheets of paper their favorite gym activities, songs learned in music, recess activities, or science experiments. Children could also select their favorite book-report projects or school lunches. From these and your own survey possibilities, choose questions that have two to five possible answers.

Decide on the Kite Attributes

Next, invite children to think about how they would like the kites to look. Have them decide on attributes for the kites, such as number of bows on the tails, length of the tails, colors of the kites, or designs on the kites. You will need the same number of attributes as you have survey questions. Assign each survey question a different attribute. (See the sample glyph survey and directions on p. 62 for suggestions.) Then let children complete their own School Year Memories Kite Glyphs.

Materials

❖ your own glyph survey and directions

❖ glyph pattern

❖ crayons or markers

❖ string, ribbon, or other supplies needed to complete your own glyph

Additional Activities

🌀 Tally the survey answers to determine students' favorite memories or activities.

🌀 Invite children to write a class letter to next year's incoming class (new class entering in the fall) telling them about their fun glyph activities this past school year. Save glyphs and children's letter to share with your new class on the first day of school.

Sample School Year Memories Kite Glyph

1. What was your favorite field trip?

	zoo	museum	aquarium
color of kite	blue	green	yellow

2. Which assembly was your favorite?

	ventriloquist	puppet show	magician
design on kite	hearts	stripes	rainbow

3. Which book report project did you enjoy the most?

	diorama	poster	book jacket
length of kite tail	4" (10 cm)	5" (13 cm)	6" (16 cm)

4. What was your favorite recess activity?

	four square	jump-rope	soccer
number of bows on tail	4	5	6

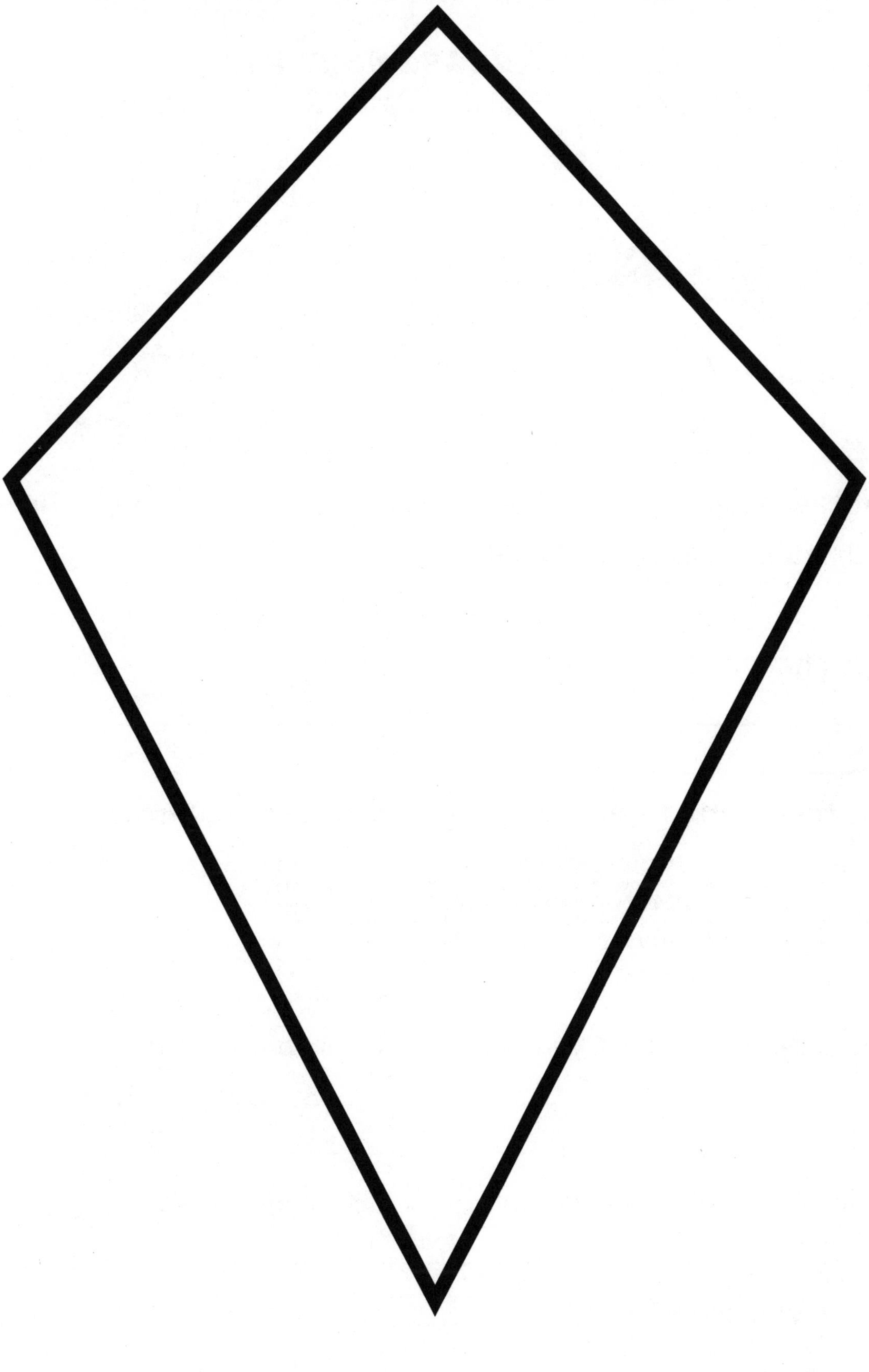

Sample Assessment Page
(based on the Pumpkin Patch Glyph, p. 22)

Kevin   Nori   Megan   José

Erica   Miguel   Shamika

Look at the pumpkin glyphs shown above to answer these questions.

1. Which students like pumpkin pie?

_____

2. Explain how you know this.

_____

_____

3. Make tally marks to show the students' favorite fall treats.

caramel apples
popcorn balls
candy corn
other

4. Write a sentence about your tally using the word *more*.

_____

_____

5. Do more students like scary or happy jack-o'-lanterns? _____

_____

6. How do you know? _____

_____

_____